972   Beck, Barbara L
Bec   73-99
        The first book of
            the Aztecs

DATE DUE		
FEB 1 0 1998		
JAN 2 9 2002		
MAY 2 9 2004		
FEB 07		
MAR 24 '10		

The First Book of the Aztecs
972 BEC   16016

Beck, Barbara L.

The FIRST BOOK of THE AZTECS

The great teocalli, *or temple, of Tenochtitlán. In the foreground is the "Wall of Serpents" and the northern entrance to this religious city. In the background is the temple dedicated to Tezcatlipoca, the "Smoking Mirror" God.*

The FIRST BOOK of
The Aztecs

:0:

by Barbara L. Beck
Pictures by Page Cary

FRANKLIN WATTS, INC.
575 Lexington Avenue, New York 10022

SBN 531-00476-7

Library of Congress Catalog Card Number: 66-18671
© Copyright 1966 by Franklin Watts, Inc.
Printed in the United States of America

6 7 8 9 10

CONTENTS

The FIRST BOOK of THE AZTECS

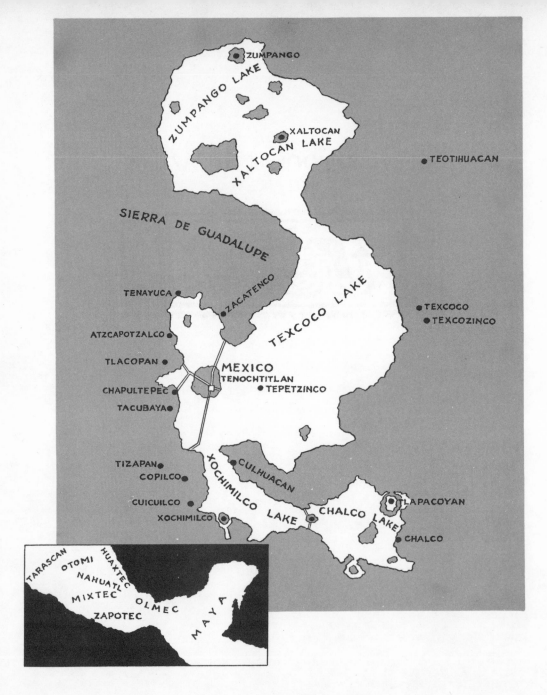

The Valley of Mexico before 1519. Inset: Important languages spoken in Mexico, and their geographic locations.

DISCOVERY

Some twenty to thirty thousand years ago, man came to the Americas from the continent of Asia. As the last great sheets of ice melted northward at the time of the earth's fourth glacial period many islands appeared in the Bering Sea. They formed an almost continuous natural land bridge between Asia and North America. In winter a mass of solid ice made the bridge complete.

For thousands of years, bands of primitive peoples came to the North American continent searching for better food-gathering, hunting, and fishing grounds. Gradually they moved south and east, following the herds of wild animals. Some of these nomads came to the Valley of Mexico between eight and ten thousand years before Christ. Here they fished in the lakes, hunted down the ancient elephants called mastodons, or killed mammoths, bison, bears, and smaller game. In addition, they gathered grains, berries, and sunflower seeds for food. Their tools were made of stone or bone, and their clothing of animal skins. Their shelters were often caves.

Many more thousands of years passed before some of these primitive peoples discovered, perhaps by accident, that plants grew from seeds poked into the ground. Sowing seeds and cultivating and harvesting plants brought a new way of life to the early farming families. Now they were able to stay in one place, build permanent shelters, and improve their cooking methods. They discovered new materials from which to make better tools and clothing. Of course, not all American Indians turned to farming. Many continued hunting and food-gathering.

I

The most important crop raised in the Valley of Mexico was Indian corn, or maize. It was first grown in the Valley some three thousand years before Christ. There, maize became the basic food, the "staff of life." Without it the Aztec civilization might never have existed.

The Valley of Mexico lies some 7,000 feet above sea level. It is surrounded by mountains, many of them volcanic. In early times the Valley was dotted with lovely lakes, which were surrounded by fertile soil. Gradually the early farmers formed communities and then, ever so slowly, worked out separate ways of living. All the people kept corn farming and the worship of nature in common, even though they developed different languages, different art and architectural styles, and different customs and dress.

Scholars now feel that the Olmec was the beginning civilization in Mexico and Central America. The Olmec people built cities at La Venta, Tres Zapotes, and San Lorenzo. Today there are Olmec ruins in the Mexican states of Tabasco and southern Vera Cruz. Here, in the thick, green jungles buzzing with insects and swarming with deadly snakes and dangerous animals, archeologists have discovered giant stone heads, some as high as eight feet and weighing up to twenty tons. These Olmec heads are known for their thick-lipped, baby-like faces.

The Olmecs understood a great deal about mathematics and astronomy and could measure the passage of time. Most scholars feel that the people of La Venta developed these sciences first and that later Central American civilizations borrowed heavily from them. The Olmecs put up stelae, large slabs of stone on which they carved

A colossal Olmec head.

hieroglyphic figures — picture writing — some of which record dates. Other carvings appear on stone doorjambs.

These same people strongly influenced their Mayan neighbors to the south; the Zapotec (*zah*-po-tek) tribes to the southwest; and the Totonac (to-to-*nahk*) people to the north.

The Olmec civilization lasted from about 800 to 400 B.C. During this time the Zapotecs became powerful. Their main ceremonial city was Monte Albán. It was built on the top of a small mountain that had been made level by huge gangs of workmen, to form a platform for the city's great temples and ball courts. To the north of the Zapotecs lived their old enemies the Mixtecs (*mee*-steks), who were famous for their goldsmithing and for their beautiful painted books, called codices.

3

The ruins of Monte Albán, the great religious center of the Zapotec people.

Over the time from the second to the seventh centuries a vigorous northern tribe built the magnificent city of Teotihuacan (tay-o-*tee*-wah-kahn). This city, three and a half miles long and nearly two miles wide, may well have been ancient Mexico's greatest. The powerful Teotihuacan civilization lasted in all for about one thousand years, and its influence was felt as far away as Guatemala.

The gigantic Temple of the Sun was built by the people of Teotihuacan. It is 215 feet high — approximately thirty stories — and was once topped by a small shrine.

The Atlantes of Tula stand on top of the pyramid to Quetzalcóatl. These warriors once helped support the roof beams of the temple. Each is armed with a dart thrower, a curved sword, and a bag of incense.

Teotihuacan was abandoned for unknown reasons in the seventh century, during a time of unrest. Many of the civilizations in the Valley had been weakened by revolt, famine, and religious problems, and were no match for the waves of energetic barbarian invaders who flooded in from the north. Finally there came a wandering people, the Toltecs, who during the ninth century founded a city called Tula. The Toltecs, the master builders of Mexico, were amazing craftsmen and clever artists and were well versed in politics. They and the later Aztecs spoke a language called Nahuatl (*nah*-wahtl).

Eventually the Toltecs' great city, Tula, was occupied by barbarians from the northwest called Chichimecs (*chee*-chee-meks),

5

"Dog People," who, it is said, ate raw meat and wore animal skins. Later a certain group of these barbarians proved themselves to be the toughest and most able warriors of the many invaders. They were called the Mexicas (*May*-hee-kahs), and later the Tenochcas (te-*notch*-kahs), "the people of Tenochtitlán (te-notch-ti-*tlahn*)." We know them today by their more popular name, the Aztecs.

The Aztecs were latecomers to the Valley of Mexico, since they arrived in the twelfth century. In a period of little more than three hundred years, from about A.D. 1200 to 1521 — when they were conquered by the Spaniards — they built a nation of tribute-paying towns and cities.

Scholars have learned about the Aztec people from the native chronicles, the picture books called codices; from the writings of the conquering Spanish soldiers; from the accounts of missionaries who came to teach the Indians after the Conquest; from the descriptions written during the sixteenth century by unknown Spanish government workers and priests; and finally, from the archeologists, who came much later and who explored and studied the remains of the past.

Only a few of the codices painted before the Spanish arrived still exist. The Spaniards destroyed the rest because they thought they were filled with magic and evil. The remaining dozen or so codices somehow found their way to several European libraries, probably because the Spaniards sent them home as curiosities.

After the Conquest the Indians quickly mastered the alphabet writing system of the Spaniards. They then wrote in their own language or in Spanish. Three of the most important post-Conquest

The people of Tula, and the Aztecs who came later, were among those who worshiped Quetzalcóatl, the plumed Serpent God. This frieze on the side of the temple to Quetzalcóatl at Xochicalco shows eight snakes winding above and below the priest-rulers of the city.

books are the *Codex Mendoza*, which deals with Aztec life and conquests; the *Codex Florentino*, which pictures Indian customs; and the *Codex Magliabecchiano*, *The Book of Life of the Ancient Mexicans*. These and other codices are filled with the Indians' history, prophecy, ritual, astronomy, songs, speeches, and general lore.

Among the most important writings of the Spanish invaders are the five letters written by Hernán Cortés, the Spanish invader, to his king, Emperor Charles V of Spain. In addition, one of Cortés' foot soldiers, Bernal Díaz del Castillo, wrote *The True History of the Conquest of New Spain* when he was about eighty-four years old. In it he recalled bloody battles, endless marches, days without food and water, and the final triumphal siege and fall of the great Aztec capital, Tenochtitlán.

The ruins of the pyramid at Tenayuca are one of the few examples of Aztec archi-tecture still standing today. If we could slice through it we would find that this is the seventh layer and that it has been built over, or enlarged, seven times. The size of the pyramid was increased at the end of each fifty-two-year period, the sacred time cycle of the Aztecs. In the foreground is Xiucóatl, "Serpent of Fire."

In 1529, eight years after the Conquest, the famous Father Bernardino de Sahagún came to Mexico. With the help of the Indians he wrote, in the native Nahuatl language, an important book, *A General History of the Affairs of New Spain.* Even today, Sahagún's reports of Indian life are of priceless value to historians.

In all, there are hundreds of accounts of life in Mexico both before and soon after the Conquest. Many later scholars have based their writings on these accounts and on the findings of the archeologists. There are over five thousand important archeological sites in Mexico. Many of them have scarcely been touched, while at others magnificent temples, broad thoroughfares, sculptures, paintings, and the tools of daily living have been found. They give us a realistic and exciting picture of the Aztecs and their way of life.

THE FORMING OF THE AZTEC NATION

The barbarian Aztecs started out from their legendary home, Aztlan, in A.D. 1168. According to some Aztec records the tribe first lived on an island in a lake. In a nearby cave one day they discovered an idol who could speak and advise them. The idol was called Huitzilopochtli (wee-tseel-o-*potch*-tlee), "Hummingbird Wizard." Huitzilopochtli told the Aztecs to search for a new land and to send pioneers ahead to plant crops that would feed the larger part of the tribe when it arrived. He also advised them not to fight and make war.

After many years of wandering, the Aztecs arrived at the forest of Chapultepec (cha-pool-tuh-*pek*), which is now a beautiful park in the heart of Mexico City. Their peaceful arrival was not even noticed by other peoples living in the Valley. Soon the Aztecs raided the city of Tenayuca (te-nah-*yoo*-kah) to steal wives for themselves, however, and war broke out. The nearby Tepanec (tay-pah-*nek*), Culhua, and Xochimilca (ho-chee-*meel*-kah) tribes attacked the Aztecs, forcing many of them to flee and taking others as slaves.

In due time the Culhuas and the Xochimilcas started warring

Aztecs hiding and weeping in the reeds along the shore of Lake Texcoco after they had been expelled from the forest of Chapultepec.

among themselves, and the Aztecs, vassals of the Culhuas, were called in to fight against the Xochimilcas. Upon winning the war, the Culhuan chief rewarded the Aztecs by giving his daughter to their chief. The Aztecs promptly sacrificed the girl. This, they thought, was the highest honor they could pay her. When the Culhuan chief arrived, expecting to attend his daughter's wedding, and discovered what had happened, he set his warriors against the Aztecs. Those who escaped the massacre fled to a miserable, swampy islet in Lake Texcoco (tess-*ko*-ko), "the Lake of the Moon."

According to some chroniclers, when Huitzilopochtli first advised his people to wander and seek a new land he also told them that they would recognize the chosen place when they saw an eagle eating a serpent while perched on a spiny cactus whose red fruits looked like human hearts. When the Aztecs arrived on the island and saw this eagle they knew that they had found their own land. The same symbol of the eagle appears on the coat of arms and flag of the Republic of Mexico today.

At first the Aztecs lived in miserable mud-and-reed huts. Fishes were plentiful in the lake, and the reed-choked swamps were filled with wild birds, frogs, and snakes. As there was almost no wood or stone on the island, the Aztecs bartered with the mainlanders for materials with which to build their town. The first building, a stone temple, was raised in 1325 in honor of Huitzilopochtli, their founding god.

The Aztecs were despised by their neighbors on the mainland, but they soon learned to provide for themselves. They built canals,

Huitzilopochtli, founding god of the Aztecs, was also the God of War, the Sun, and Hunting.

bridges, and causeways over the marshes — even to nearby islands. They learned to make rafts of reeds, which they covered with mud and anchored in the marshes or along the edges of nearby islands. The mud rafts were then planted with vegetables. These floating gardens, called *chinampas* (chee-*nam*-pahs), greatly increased the amount of gardening land. The rich lake-bottom mud used in *chinampa* farming produced luxuriant crops. *Chinampas* can still be seen today, south of Mexico City at a place called the Floating Gardens of Xochimilco.

Gradually the Aztecs turned their swampy, snake-infested island into a place of abundance. When more room for living was needed,

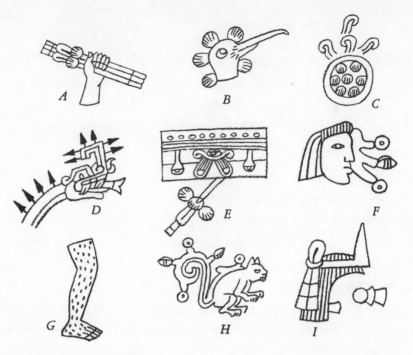

Hieroglyphs of the Aztec rulers: A. Acamapichtli. B. Huitzilhuitl. C. Chimalpopoca. D. Itzcóatl. E. Montezuma I. F. Axayacatl. G. Tizoc. H. Ahuitzotl. I. Montezuma II. (From the Codex Mendoza.*)*

the *chinampa* garden areas were filled in and the space was used for new houses. The people called their city Tenochtitlán.

At about this time one group of Aztecs broke away from the others and started building a twin city on a nearby islet. They called it Tlaltelolco (tlal-tel-*ol*-ko). A bridge separated the sister cities, which were rivals for many years, partly because Tlaltelolco had a bigger marketplace and the Tenochcas were jealous. Eventually Tlaltelolco was conquered, the water between the cities was filled in, and Tlaltelolco became a part of Tenochtitlán.

The Tepanecs, a people to whom the Aztecs already paid tribute, began to notice the achievements of these island people, and they set an impossible tribute on them. The Aztecs were required to bring living trees in full bloom, a beautiful floating garden, and ducks that would lay eggs the moment they reached the Tepanecs. Again, it is said, Huitzilopochtli appeared before his unhappy people and promised help. Somehow the Aztecs were able to deliver the living trees and gardens, and when the Tepanec king reached for a duck it laid eggs right in his hand.

The early history of the Aztecs is filled with minor struggles, intrigue, alliances, broken alliances, and full-scale wars with their mainland neighbors. Finally, under the brilliant leadership of their king, Itzcóatl (eets-*ko*-atl), the Aztecs began taking over scores of small city-states in the Valley. Itzcóatl's death in 1440 brought to the throne another remarkable king, Montezuma I, who was also known as Ilhuicamina (eel-wee-kah-*meen*-ah), "the Wrathful." Montezuma I fought and defeated the Chalca tribe. His powerful armies also crossed the mountains to the east of the Valley to raid tribes living near the Gulf of Mexico at a distance of about two hundred miles.

In addition to being an able military leader, Montezuma I took an interest in the welfare of his people. It was during his reign, and with the help of the outstanding Nezahualcoyotl (ne-za-wal-*koy*-otl), king of the Texcocans, that an aqueduct was built to bring sweet water from springs three miles away in the forest of Chapultepec. On the eastern edge of Tenochtitlán the two great leaders

This reconstruction of Tenochtitlán's inner religious city shows the temple-pyramid of Huitzilopochtli and Tlaloc, the Rain God. The circular temple in the foreground is dedicated to Quetzalcóatl. It is round because the Aztecs believed that this would please the wind.

also had a twelve-mile-long dike constructed, to control the spread of the lake water during the rainy seasons.

In 1469, Axayacatl (ash-ay-*ah*-katl) succeeded his father, Montezuma I. For the next ten years the Aztecs increased their domain westward and southward. Axayacatl also led his people against the Tarascans, but was badly defeated. The Tarascans remained independent until the arrival of the Spaniards.

In 1479, Axayacatl died of a wound he had received several years before during a battle. His brother Tizoc, "Bloodstained Leg," succeeded him. Tizoc's reign ended in 1486 when he was poisoned by his own lords, who claimed he was a cowardly military leader.

Tizoc's brother Ahuitzotl (ah-*weet*-sotl), "Water Dog," came to the throne and proved himself a forceful ruler. The combined armies of the Tenochcans and Texcocans swept down on the peoples north of present-day Oaxaca (wah-*hah*-ka) — the Mixtecs and the Zapotecs. The two-year campaign produced no less than twenty thousand prisoners. They were brought back to Tenochtitlán and lined up in two rows. The two victorious kings set about the task of slashing open the captured victims' chests, snatching out their hearts, and offering them to the gods. Needless to say, the ceremony went on for days, and lesser lords in turn took over the grisly task.

Ahuitzotl sent his armies as far as the Pacific Ocean, south to Guatemala, and east to the Atlantic Ocean. In addition, his soldiers were constantly called upon to put down the revolts of previously conquered tribes.

In 1503 a flood caused by torrential rains broke the dam built by Nezahualcoyotl and Montezuma I. Some scholars think that

The Stone of Tizoc records the conquests of this king. He is shown grasping the hair of a prisoner — a sign of a victory.

Ahuitzotl died from being hit by a stone while he was supervising repairs on the dam. He was succeeded by his nephew, Montezuma II, in 1503. This powerful ruler overran his former allies, the Texcocans, and captured some forty-three towns in the Oaxaca area. About twelve thousand prisoners from the Oaxaca campaigns were sacrificed to the gods under the direction of Montezuma II.

While new conquests were going forward around Oaxaca, news came that white men in strange boats had been seen along the Mayan coast, in what is now Yucatán. Two years later, in 1519, the Spanish conquistador Hernán Cortés started his march from the Gulf Coast to Tenochtitlán.

THE AZTECS, PEOPLE OF THE SUN

By the time Cortés arrived in Mexico, the warlike Aztec kings had led their armies of farmer-warriors to great power. Tenochtitlán controlled the territory of almost one-half modern-day Mexico and received tribute from its people. What were these farmer-warriors like? How did they live when they were not at war?

The average citizen was perhaps five feet, two or three inches tall. His complexion was a bronzy brown; his eyes and hair were black. Men wore their hair long and in bangs. Because the Aztecs, like all American Indians, had very little hair on their faces, shaving was uncommon.

Aztec men wore a *maxtli* (*mash*-tlee), or loincloth. This garment was wrapped around the waist, passed between the legs, and tied in front. For the common people the *maxtli* was of plain white cotton. Cotton was grown in the hot lands to the east and west of the Valley of Mexico. A white cloak called a *tilmantli* (teel-*man*-tlee) was made of fiber from the agave plant, or from cotton. This rectangular cloak was tied over the right shoulder or across the chest.

Aztec women. (From the Codex Florentino.)

As Tenochtitlán's climate was moderate, with warm, mostly sunny, days and cool nights, the loincloth and cloak were all the clothing a man needed.

Aztec women wore an ankle-length skirt called a *cueitl* (ƙway-tl). This piece of cloth was wrapped around the body and held by an embroidered belt at the waist. There were no hooks and eyes, buttons, or snaps in early Mexico. In addition, a woman wore a *huipilli* (wee-*peel*-lee), a kind of long blouse with slits for the head and arms. This was pulled on over the head. Women often wore two or three skirts and blouses of varying lengths, one over the other. They wore their hair long and straight or, when they worked in the fields, twined around their heads.

The everyday clothing of the common people was white, but for special occasions both men and women wore colorful embroidered clothing. On those special days, too, instead of going barefoot they wore sandals called *cactli*, (ƙaƙ-tlee). These sandals were made of animal hides or agave fibers and were held on by crisscross straps.

Noble families dressed the same as the commoners except that their clothing was finer, and beautifully embroidered in brilliant designs. Their sandals were sometimes made of jaguar skins or were painted turquoise blue or decorated with precious stones and gold.

Both the men and the women of the nobility wore jewelry: necklaces, earrings, and arm and ankle bracelets. The noblemen pierced their noses and wore jewels in them. They also made a hole beneath their lower lip and filled it with ornaments of gold, turquoise, shell, or crystal. Not everyone could wear what he wanted, however. It depended upon one's social standing. For example, only the king could wear a turquoise ornament in his nose.

The lords of the realm also wore cloaks and magnificent headdresses made of feathers. The most prized feathers were those from the rare quetzal bird found in the Guatemalan highlands.

The Aztecs' day began before dawn with the blowing of conch shells and the beating of great drums atop the temple-pyramids. Women rose and rekindled their fires. Men went out to the *temascalli,* the steam bath close by their houses. The *temascalli* was a round little building of stone and cement. Outside one wall a fire was lighted, and when the stones were sufficiently hot, the bather crept into the building through a small low door and threw water on the inside of this wall. Soon the tiny building was filled with steam, and the bather switched himself with long grasses in place of scrubbing. If a commoner did not have a *temascalli,* he bathed in a nearby canal or in the lake that nearly surrounded Tenochtitlán. The Aztecs were clean people. They did not have soap, but they did have two plants that produced soaplike substances, one from its fruits and the other from its roots.

Meanwhile the women of the family were busily boiling maize,

then grinding it in *metates* (me-*tah*-tays) — hollowed-out slabs of stone. The *metate* held the maize while a kind of rolling pin called a *mano* was worked back and forth to crush the corn. The maize was then patted into large, round, flat cakes and cooked over the fire in a *comalli*, a flat clay cooking plate. These maize cakes, called *tortillas* (tor-*tee*-yas) by the Spaniards, were eaten every day.

Usually the men left at dawn, without breakfast. In Tenochtitlán they poled their dugouts along the canals to their fields or *chinampas,* the floating gardens. At about ten o'clock in the morning they drank a bowl of nourishing *atolli*, a corn gruel that was sometimes sweetened with honey or spiced with pimento. By midafternoon the farmers returned for their main meal of the day. The men of the house took their meals squatting on mats called *petatls* (pe-

tah-tls), which were placed around the hearth. Women and children ate separately from the men.

The Aztecs ate maize cakes, many kinds of beans, sweet potatoes, peppers, avocados, tomatoes, squashes, fishes, and on special occasions, meat. But meat was scarce, and the only kinds available to the common people were turkeys, and perhaps ducks, and small hairless dogs that were raised for food. In the homes of the lords, however, a wide variety of meats was served: turkey, rabbit, deer, duck, pheasant, quail, partridge, wild boar, and the small dog. In addition, the aristocrats imported from the hot lands near the Atlantic and Pacific coasts such luxuries as vanilla, chocolate, tropical fruits of all kinds, and tobacco for smoking.

Because the Aztecs were lake people they ate things that were found in or near water: fishes, frogs, freshwater shrimps, worms, water flies, and snakes.

Night falls fast in Mexico, and in the fading light of day and by firelight, men sharpened or mended their farming, hunting, and fishing tools. Women busied themselves with sewing, spinning thread, weaving with a backstrap loom, and preparing corn for the next day. With the sound of conchs and great drums in the temples the day came to an end. Grass mats were unrolled and placed on a raised level of earth in the houses, and everyone went to bed. For, according to Sahagún, the Aztec day was marked by nine time divisions. The conchs and drums sounded at sunrise, midmorning, noon, sunset, the beginning of night, bedtime, the time for prayers by the priests, a time shortly after midnight, and rising time, a little before dawn.

The Aztec farmer needed to work his lands only 200 days out of the 365-day year in order to produce some 200 bushels of corn. As this was more corn than his family needed, he used the surplus to pay his taxes or to barter for weapons, clothing, meat, or whatever caught his eye in the marketplace. But because the soil became exhausted after two years — two crops — it was necessary for a part of the *milpa*, the cornfield, to lie idle for ten years before it could be used again. Accordingly, the average family had about ten acres of land, but only a small portion was planted each year.

The land was not owned by the farmer, but was loaned to him by the *calpullec,* (kal-*pul*-lek), the chief of the *calpulli*. In the early days of the Aztecs a *calpulli* was a sort of clan made up of blood-related families. But at the height of the Aztec rule a *calpulli* became more like one of our political districts.

All lands were divided up and parceled out to each household. If a farmer died without heirs, the land went back to the *calpulli*, to be distributed again. Generally the *calpullec* allowed the parcel to remain with the family, however. A lazy farmer or one who produced poor crops lost his land.

To prepare a new *milpa* the Aztec farmers first had to fell trees with stone axes. The trees were then burned, and the wood ashes were used to fertilize and loosen the soil. Later the farmers used a *coa*, a digging stick, to turn over the earth and to make holes in the ground for the kernels of maize at plantingtime. Between the rows of maize the farmers planted beans and squashes. In addition to these and many other vegetables the Aztecs planted flowers; they loved flowers.

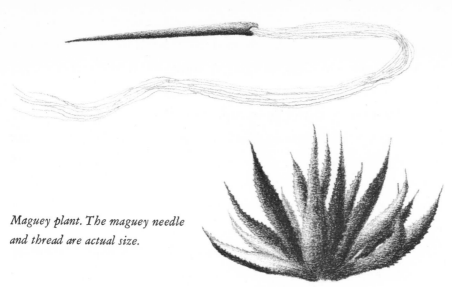

*Maguey plant. The maguey needle
and thread are actual size.*

One of the most important plants native to Mexico was the agave
or maguey (ma-*gay*). Its large, thick blades were used for roofing
huts. After being beaten and dried, the blades yielded fibers for
making clothing or rope. At the end of each blade is a spine like a
needle, and when this was bitten or cut at the base in a certain way
it was released, bringing along its own fibers of thread, ready for
sewing.

Peeled maguey blades produced sheets of thin paper suitable for
writing. Finally, when the plant's center was cut out, a core or heart
which contained sap was revealed. This was fermented to make a
cidery-tasting beer called *octli* by the Indians. Drinking was
frowned on in Aztec times, and the punishments for public drunk-
enness ranged from having one's head shaved to being beaten or
strangled to death. *Octli* was drunk, therefore, only on special family and religious occasions. Old people also were allowed to drink
it, for they were no longer considered useful to society.

A typical Aztec farmer's house.

In addition to being farmers, the Aztecs were hunters and fishermen. Birds were brought down with stone pellets from blowguns; small animals were caught in traps; fishes were caught in nets thrown from dugouts. Only the aristocracy was allowed to hunt with bows and arrows for larger game such as deer, as these animals had almost all been killed off in the Valley of Mexico.

The houses of the common people generally had only one room, with a partition that separated the sleeping area from the living-eating area. The walls were built of reeds and mud. The roof was a thatching of reeds and grasses, and the floor was packed earth. There were no windows and only one doorway. In contrast, the higher classes and nobles lived in adobe — sun-dried clay brick — or stone houses with many rooms and doors arranged around a rectangular inner court planted with flower and vegetable gardens. These houses were usually painted white.

The work-filled day of the Aztec family would have been monotonous had it not been for occasional games. One popular game was called *patolli*. Players used a board shaped like a cross, divided into fifty-two squares. Beans marked with spots were used as dice, and colored stones were used as the men on the board. The beans were thrown, and the player moved his colored stone from square to

The ruins of the ball court at Monte Albán, religious city of the Zapotec people.

square for as many spots as had been shown on the beans. The winner was the player who returned "home" first.

Another game, played only by the nobles, was called *tlachtli* (*tlatch*-tlee). It was a popular spectator sport. Two teams in a court shaped like a capital I tried to make a solid rubber ball about six inches in diameter go into the opposing team's part of the court. In addition, there were two stone rings placed vertically on facing walls in the center of the court. If a player could pass the ball through a ring, his team automatically won. But this seldom happened, as the ball could only be struck with the knees, elbows, and hips. The players were well padded and wore leather gloves to prevent bruises and cuts. As the Aztecs loved gambling, betting ran high at these ball games. Gold, slaves, clothing, even houses and land, changed hands. If a team was able to put the ball through one of the two rings, both the winning players and the bettors were permitted to snatch the clothing from the backs of the losers.

These two games, *patolli* and *tlachtli*, had religious meaning. The cross-shaped board and the fifty-two squares represented the four chief directions of the gods and the length of the Aztec religious time period; the rubber ball used in *tlachtli* was a symbol of the sun. For the Aztecs almost everything had religious meaning.

EDUCATION AND THE SOCIAL CLASSES

The moment a child was born, his parents consulted a priest, who looked in the *tonalamatl* (to-*nah*-la-*mah*-tl), the book of fate, to see if the day was lucky or unlucky. If the day had an unlucky sign, the child would not be named until the priest found a day with a better omen. If the day of birth was lucky, the child was named at a family ceremony that took place four days later. It was thought that babies born under the day-sign 1 *ocelotl* (os-e-*lo*-tl) would die as prisoners of war, for example, whereas a child born on 1 *calli* might become a successful doctor.

Children were given unusual and striking names. A boy might be named Chimalpopoca, which means "Smoking Shield"; Itz-cóatl, which means "Obsidian Snake"; or Nezahualcoyotl, which means "Hungry Coyote." He might instead be named for the date of his birth — for instance, Ce Acatl, which means "One Reed." Girls were often given names that ended with the word, "flower,"

An Aztec mother teaches her daughter to grind corn in a metate. *Note the speech scroll near the mother's mouth. This indicates that she is talking. (From the* Codex Mendoza.)

xochitl, such as Quiauhxochitl, "Rain Flower," or Matlalxochitl, "Green Flower."

Children's education began at the age of three, when their parents lectured them on the importance of duty and of working hard and leading a good life. The *Codex Mendoza* shows, in a series of pictures, that a three-year-old was given one-half a maize cake each day. Four- and five-year-olds were given one maize cake a day. Between the ages of six and twelve a child received one and a half maize cakes, and from thirteen on, two maize cakes a day. Of course, children also ate other things, such as vegetables, fish, and occasionally meat. The rationing was probably part of the strict discipline that children had to endure.

From the ages of three to six a child was expected to do small household chores and to fetch and carry things for his parents. Disobedient children might be pricked with maguey needles or left tied and naked in a mud puddle overnight. From the age of six on, boys learned farming, fishing, or their father's trade, while girls were taught by their mothers.

When a boy was twelve, according to some authorities, or when he was somewhere between the ages of six and nine, according to others, he was expected to attend the clan's school, the *telpuchcalli* (*tel*-pootch-*kahl*-lee), or House of Youth. The *telpuchcalli* offered standard training in citizenship, religious ritual, history and tradition, arts and crafts, and the use of weapons. As many of the teachers were soldiers who had earned the right to teach by capturing prisoners in battle, the emphasis in the school was on the use of weapons and on war.

According to Sahagún, life at the *telpuchcalli* was rough. Although the boys were allowed to go home for meals and to learn their father's work, they were made to sleep at school, sweep the temple steps, keep the sacred fires going, cut wood for the school, do farm work, repair and construct buildings, canals, roads, and ditches, and generally help the priests. All the while, they were learning the art of warfare. When the army went to war, these young men journeyed along too, and served as squires to warriors in battle.

In the evening, after school, according to Sahagún, they returned home, bathed, painted their bodies, and went to the Cuicacalli (*kwee*-ka-*kahl*-lee), the House of Song. There they sang and danced until midnight.

Boys being taken to the calmecac *by their fathers. (From the* Codex Flor-entino.)

When a *telpuchcalli* student captured his first enemy he was allowed to cut off a braid he had worn on the back of his head up to that time. In addition, he could leave school. A boy who failed to bring back a prisoner after several battles, however, was considered a disgrace. He, too, could leave school, but would never be able to hold any office or wear fine clothes. Boys were also allowed to leave the *telpuchcalli* when they wished to marry and take up farming or a trade.

In addition to the *tepuchcalli* there were several temple or monastery schools called *calmecacs* (*kahl*-may-*kahks*). These schools were attended by the sons of nobles. The higher education offered in the *calmecacs* prepared young men to become priests and chiefs.

If life was hard at the *telpuchcalli*, it was even harder at the *calmecac*. In addition to performing all the duties required of the boys at the *telpuchcalli*, *calmecac* students were taught manners, discipline, self-control, and self-denial. At night, for instance, they

Featherworkers tied the stems of feathers into fabrics during the weaving process. They produced brilliant geometric designs and richly colored landscapes. (From the Codex Florentino.*)*

would rise and go into the mountains to burn incense to the gods. There they pricked their legs and ears with maguey spines and offered the blood to the gods. Often, on other nights, these young men rose and bathed in the freezing lake waters. They were expected to fast and do penance. Punishment for not greeting and speaking politely to others was severe. The school built strong character and stout bodies that could withstand suffering and pain. The priests taught the young students history, the holy songs written in their books, reading and writing, astrology, counting time, and the interpretation of dreams. A *calmecac* student was expected to have all the knowledge known to the Aztecs and to be heroic in battle.

Aztec girls had the same two choices of schooling, but their schools were run by priestesses. Discipline was just as strict. The girls' *calmecac* trained young women to become priestesses or the wives of high-ranking officials. They were instructed in manners, religious ritual, fine weaving, and featherwork.

Although both young men and young women could elect to stay in the *calmecac* all their lives, most chose marriage. If a young man wished to be released from either the *calmecac* or the *telpuchcalli*, his family had to invite the school's masters to an elaborate feast. Following this, the elders of the family presented a polished stone ax to the masters and asked for the boy's discharge. When the masters accepted the ax and left the house, the boy was free of further schooling and could marry.

Before marriage, as at birth, priest-diviners studied the omens and signs under which the bride-to-be was born. These signs were compared, almost always favorably, with the boy's birth signs. Marriages were arranged by the boy's parents. Old women were called in to act as go-betweens with the girl's family. After much dickering and polite refusals the marriage was settled upon, and the soothsayer was again called upon to set a day for the wedding, which must take place under good signs.

The night before the marriage a huge feast was held at the bride's house. Before this she was bathed and her legs and arms were adorned with red feathers. The next evening her future husband's relatives led the gay marriage procession through the streets to his house. The bride was often carried on the back of an old woman. There was much singing and dancing, and when the group had entered the house, the bride and groom sat on mats before the hearth. After many speeches by the elders the groom's cloak was tied to the girl's blouse. This was the symbol of their marriage. The wedding party then ate large quantities of food and drink.

31

Aztec marriage ceremony. (From the Codex Mendoza.)

Once married, a man received his plot of land from the *calpullec,* head chief of the *calpulli.* Under this chief were various officers, who were overseers of public works and tax collecting, and of groups of families. During the days of Montezuma II much of the power passed to the top layer of the ruling classes, called the *tecuhtli* (tay-*koo*-tlee). The king, his four mighty warlords, and the highest ranking nobles were the *tecuhtli.* At one time these

An Aztec noble. (From the Codex Florentino.)

An Aztec ruler sitting on the royal petatl, *or* mat. *(From the* Codex Mendoza.)

officials were elected by the people, but later they were appointed by the king.

The *tecuhtli* lords were responsible for their people: they maintained law and order, acted as judges during lawsuits, saw to the cultivation of the land, and led their people in battle. The members of the *tecuhtli* lived in palaces built and maintained by the people, enjoyed the produce from the lands worked by the commoners, and were often awarded clothing and food by the king. Battalions of lesser government officials helped keep records, settle disputes, and file reports.

In a country that was constantly at war, the way to gain office, power, prestige, and riches was to distinguish oneself in battle. When an Aztec warrior killed or captured four of the enemy, he was given the title *tequiua* (tay-kee-*oo*-ah), which meant "one who has (a share of) tribute." Even if he was a commoner he automatically became a member of the nobility, with the rank of commander and the right to sit in on war councils. Each time he distinguished himself in battle he received more honors, a greater share of the wealth, and the command of a larger group of war-

Because the pochteca *frequently had to fight for their lives, they traveled fully armed. (From the* Codex Mendoza.*)*

riors. In addition, with each increase in rank he wore a more elaborate uniform. A commoner, then, could become a member of the nobility. This merit system helped strengthen the Aztec people because it constantly made it possible for brave, able, and ambitious men to move to positions of command.

Next on the social ladder beneath the *tecuhtli* and the lesser nobles were the *pochteca* (potch-*tay*-kah), the merchant class. The fearless *pochteca* ranged many hundreds of miles from Tenochtitlán and were useful spies, as they often traded in enemy territory. They brought back to the king reports on the strengths and weaknesses of unconquered provinces.

The *pochteca* lived in a certain part of each city, had their own

Slaves carried the poch-
*teca's goods on their
backs, using tumplines,
bands that went around
the forehead and helped
bear the weight of the
load. (From the* Codex
Mendoza.*)*

special god — Yacatecuhtli (*ya*-kah-te-*koo*-tlee), "Lord Who Guides" — their own judges, and their own banner when they went to war.

By the time the Spaniards arrived, the children of the merchant class could attend *calmecacs,* the schools of the nobility. But the merchants were careful never to flaunt their ever increasing wealth and power in front of the jealous nobility. In fact, the *pochteca* generally went about in simple clothing, because the nobles disdained a man who put personal gain before glory on the battlefield.

There were no pack animals in Mexico before the arrival of the Spaniards, who brought horses. Although Aztec wheeled toys have been found, the Indians did not really understand how a wheel could be used for transport, and everything was carried on people's backs. The *pochteca* used slaves to carry their goods.

Merchants arrived from their long, dangerous trips secretly and

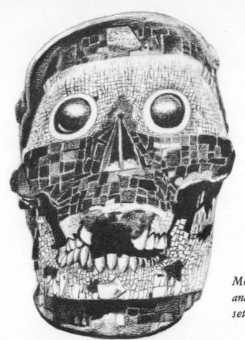

Mosaic mask. Turquoise and lignite have been set into a human skull.

at night. They unloaded their packs of cotton, cacao, rubber, jade, pottery, feathers, nuts, herbs, medicines, and chicle — the gum of the sapodilla tree which produces chewing gum — and often stored them under the name of a relative or friend. When the merchants left on another trading trip, the members of their families took a vow to wash their faces only once every four months until their return. Merchants often departed on the day *1 coatl* (1 snake), as this was considered a very lucky day.

In the class below the *pochteca* were the *tolteca,* or craftsmen, so named because they were thought to be the direct descendants of the ancient master builders in the Valley of Mexico, the Toltecs. The clever, highly skilled *tolteca* worked in gold, silver, turquoise, amber, pearls, amethysts, shells, feathers, wood, and stone. A father

Slaves of the Aztecs, as pictured in the Codex Florentino.

taught his son his craft and on occasion taught the young sons of the nobility. Although the *tolteca* paid taxes, they were not called upon to work on public projects.

The common people made up the next class. They were the *macehualtin*, (*mah*-se-*wahl*-teen). They worked their land, paid taxes, fought in the army, and when called upon, cleaned, maintained, and built roads, canals, bridges, and temples, and performed other public works. They could be summoned at any time to work on community projects.

Below the *macehualtin* in social standing were the *tlalmaitl* (tlal-*mah*-eetl), a class of tenant farmers. These people were not allowed to be citizens or own land. They worked the fields of some dignitary to whom they paid rent. They also acted as his servants. The *tlalmaitl* neither paid taxes nor served on community projects, but they did do military service.

At the bottom of Aztec society were the slaves. A slave, or *tlacotli* (tla-*ko*-tlee), was neither free nor a citizen. He belonged to his master. Strangely enough, a slave could have money and own things. He could even have his own slaves, and he could buy himself out of slavery. A slave was treated kindly. He was fed, clothed, and housed as well as any common citizen. If he escaped in the marketplace, he could be chased only by his master or his master's sons. If he could reach the king's palace before he was caught, he was free from then on. If anyone besides his owner's family gave chase, that person automatically became a slave.

Slaves were sometimes prisoners of war who had been saved from the sacrificial altars, or they were part of a tribute paid by some conquered province. During hard times a free citizen could sell himself into slavery if he so chose. After being paid something like twenty pieces of cloth, the slave-to-be remained free until he had spent this pay, then he began his servitude. If a slave was lazy or thieving and because of this had been sold two times to different masters, his fate was sealed. He was then sold for the last time, in the marketplace, to be sacrificed.

WAR AND RELIGION

The word "sacrifice" is the key to Aztec religion. The Aztecs believed that when the sun set, it began a nightlong battle with the powers of darkness. In order that it might be reborn — that is, rise each morning — it must be fed human blood; otherwise, the world would come to an end. As the chosen people of Huitzilopochtli, the Aztecs believed that they had the divine mission of keeping the Sun God alive with blood sacrifices.

Human victims to be sacrificed were taken mostly on the field of

A priest plucks out the heart of a victim and sacrifices it to the sun. (From the Codex Florentino.)

battle. One purpose of war, then, was to secure prisoners — not to kill and plunder. The Aztecs even invented "Wars of Flowers" in which they engaged their neighbors in ceremonial battle. The time, place, and number of warriors were agreed upon before the battle. The object was to capture as many prisoners as possible. During one "War of Flowers" with the Cholulans, the Aztecs, having captured enough prisoners, even sent an emissary to see if the Cholulans were satisfied. When word came back that they were, both armies packed up and took their prisoners home to the sacrificial altars.

According to several Spanish chroniclers, many thousands of persons were offered to the gods each year. During a severe drought and famine in the mid-fifteenth century the Aztecs sacrificed as many as ten thousand victims. When the famine ended, the Aztecs

39

were sure that they had pleased the gods, so they continued the awful bloodletting.

But war was not waged solely for religious reasons. The Aztecs felt that they had a divine right to rule in the Valley of Mexico because they were the direct descendants of the Toltecs, former masters of central Mexico. As Tenochtitlán grew to be the greatest power in the Valley and the population increased, the need for land and goods became greater.

When the Aztecs conquered new lands they did not remain to rule them. The defeated peoples kept their own leaders, but were obliged to pay tribute to Tenochtitlán. The Aztec nation was not an empire, but a loose federation of tribute-paying towns and cities.

The Aztecs had a favorite excuse for going to war. If a *pochteca*, or merchant, was robbed, attacked, or uncivilly treated while on a trading trip, the king and his council declared war. Since the merchants were used as spies and were even instructed to provoke an unpleasant incident occasionally, it must have been hard for neighboring countries to be hospitable.

Whatever the reasons for war — broken trade routes, political disagreements, or some trivial incident — the Aztecs always tried first to negotiate. Politics were carried on in a courtly fashion. Ambassadors carrying threats and entreaties were sent to the rebellious city. If talk failed, the arrogant ambassadors returned once more to call on the enemy ruler. They plastered his right arm and head with gum and feathers, placed a feathered headdress on his head, and presented him with weapons. Even after this amazing insult they were allowed to leave the city alive.

Following the ambassadors' report to the Aztec king, he called in his councillors and the four great generals representing the quarters of the kingdom. Word was sent out, and a priest danced through the streets with a rattle and shield, announcing the war. Next the war drums sounded and the warriors assembled at the *tlacochcalco* (*tla*-kotch-*kal*-ko), "the house of darts" or arsenal, which was located next to the great temple.

The fighting men wore quilted cotton suits soaked in brine to make them stiff. These suits covered the whole body and were nearly as effective as a suit of armor. The great chiefs wore on their backs huge wooden frames ornamented with brilliant feathers. Magnificent plumed headdresses, shields painted in a rainbow of colors, and feathered or multicolored cloaks were worn according to rank. The noblest warrior classes, the Eagle Knights and the Jaguar Knights, had special insignia. The Jaguar Knights wore the skins of the jaguar in battle, and the Eagle Knights wore helmets shaped like an eagle's head. Other helmets, made of reeds, bone, feathers, paper, cloth, and wood, were made to resemble tigers, pumas, and snakes.

An advance party of captains and their bravest warriors left the great square first. A day later the priests, with idols strapped to their backs, set out. On the third day the main army began its march in orderly silence. Women went along to cook and to carry supplies. Because it was difficult to feed such a huge force, most battles lasted only a few days.

When the battleground was reached, the enemy ruler was called in for a final conference. If this failed, a huge bonfire was lighted,

An Aztec warrior in full battle dress. A wooden frame on his back is decorated with waving plumes.

onto which incense was thrown. This was the signal of war. Taking their battle stations, the warriors began whistling, howling, sounding drums and conch shells, and banging their weapons against their shields. In this deafening noise the first squads took to the field. They were archers armed with bows and arrows, and slingsmen who hurled stones from slings. Next came the lance or dart throwers. Lances were from six to ten feet long and were decorated with feathers and paper. The tips were of obsidian, a hard volcanic glass that was razor-sharp. Obsidian-tipped darts were hurled with great force by means of throwers called *atlatls* (aht-*lah*-tls). An *atlatl* was a short wooden staff with a middle groove, and a peg at one end against which the dart fitted. When the *atlatl* was thrust forward quickly, it let the lance go with more momentum than merely throwing it by hand would have.

Hand-to-hand fighters used sword-clubs called *maquahuitls* (*mah*-kwa-*wee*-tls), which were toothed with obsidian blades. The Spaniards found that these sword-clubs were so deadly they could sever a horse's head in one blow. The Aztec shields were made of wooden wickerwork covered with animal hide. They were decorated with paint or feathers, and usually bore the emblem of the clan to which the owner belonged.

The Aztecs depended more on sheer weight of numbers than on tactics. When the main temple in the enemy's city had been taken, the war came to an end. The victorious Aztecs then sent a runner to Tenochtitlán with his hair braided. He joyously waved a sword-club as he entered the city. But if the Aztecs lost, the runner entered the city silently, wearing his hair over his face.

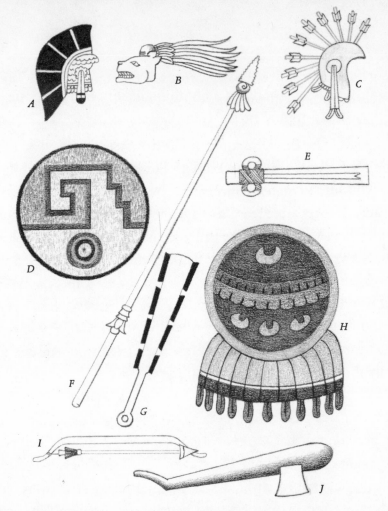

A, B, C. Headdresses of warriors; D. Feathered shield. E. Atlatl, a dart thrower.
F. Spear. G. Maquahuitl, a sword-club; H. Shield; I. Bow and arrow. J. Club with a
single blade.

From the moment he was born, an Aztec warrior was dedicated to battle. If he died in combat or was sacrificed to the sun by the enemy, he would go to a special East Paradise, according to the Aztec belief. Here all warriors gathered with their shields and lances to conduct the sun to its zenith each day. After four years a warrior returned to earth as a hummingbird to live in warm, sun-filled gardens, sipping nectar from flowers.

The Aztecs believed in three separate worlds: the heavens, of which there were thirteen; the world of man; and the underworlds, which numbered nine. Each heaven had its own characteristics. For example, in the Fifth Heaven, fire and fire snakes, comets, and stars wandered about. In the Eighth Heaven, obsidian-edged knives clashed constantly and there were storms. According to their importance, the various gods lived in different levels of the heavens.

When a person died he went to one of the paradises or to the underworld, Mictlan (*meek*-tlan). The four-year journey to Mictlan was filled with many horrors. A dead soul had to avoid such things as two mountains that kept crashing together, a snake, and an alligator. He had to endure the hardships of eight deserts, and freezing winds that hurled obsidian knives. Finally the traveler

Mitla is east of present-day Oaxaca. It was once thought that it stood over the entrance to Mictlan, the Aztec underworld.

reached a wide river, which he crossed by riding on the back of a little red dog. Upon reaching the Lord of the Dead and giving him gifts, the dead soul was assigned to one of the nine layers of the underworld.

In addition to dividing the universe vertically into heavens, earth, and underworlds, the Aztecs divided it horizontally into directions: north, south, east, and west. Each area was believed to be controlled by certain gods.

The great gods of the Aztecs were Huitzilopochtli, God of War and the Sun, and the founding god of the Aztecs; Tezcatlipoca (tes-kaht-*lee*-po-ka), "Smoking Mirror," chief god of the pantheon; and Quetzalcóatl (kayt-zahl-*ko*-atl), "Feathered Serpent," God of Life and Learning, and of the Wind. In addition, the Aztecs worshiped Tlaloc, the principal rain god; Coatlicue (ko-at-*lee*-kway), the mother goddess; the maguey-plant goddess, Mayahuel; a corn god and goddess; gods of earth, death, water, sky, planets, stars, birds, animals, and many, many others.

Aztec gods and goddesses had dual natures. That is, they could be good or evil. An army of priests and priestesses was needed to serve this host of deities, interpret their moods, and win their favor. The two highest priests lived in Tenochtitlán. Under them were priests who were in charge of the worship of each of the many gods and goddesses. Other priests had charge of incoming tribute, and still others managed the priests' schools. Below these were thousands of lesser priests who read signs, predicted future events, healed the sick, taught, and officiated at the many ceremonies.

The main priestly duty, however, was conducting sacrifices. A victim who was to die on the altar wore fine clothing and was held

The hideous goddess Coatlicue, "the Lady of the Serpent Skirts." This stone sculpture, over eight feet tall, weighs about twelve tons and was found in 1790 beneath the main square of Mexico City.

in high esteem, for it was thought that he was the representative of the god to whom he was sacrificed. After a prisoner's heart had been plucked out or he had been flayed or beheaded, the priests smeared his blood on the idol of the god and on their own hair. According to Díaz del Castillo they wore black robes and their hair was "very long and so matted that it could not be separated or disentangled . . . and it was clotted with blood." The priests stained their bodies black, and pricked their earlobes so often with maguey needles that they were shredded. Their lives were stern, and were spent in fasting, praying, and burning incense.

47

THE ACHIEVEMENTS OF THE AZTECS

In addition to serving the gods, the priests were the intellectual leaders of the Aztecs. They taught time counting, picture writing, mathematics, astronomy, astrology, medicine, history, songs, and dancing.

Like the people before them in the Valley, the Aztecs understood time. Their calendar, called the *tonalpohualli* (to-*nahl*-po-*wahl*-lee), or "count of days," was figured by adding the numbers 1 to 13 to 20

The Aztec day-signs. 1. Crocodile. 2. Wind. 3. House. 4. Lizard. 5. Serpent. 6. Death's-head. 7. Deer. 8. Rabbit. 9. Water. 10. Dog. 11. Monkey. 12. Grass. 13. Reed. 14. Ocelot. 15. Eagle. 16. Vulture. 17. Motion. 18. Flint knife. 19. Rain. 20. Flower.

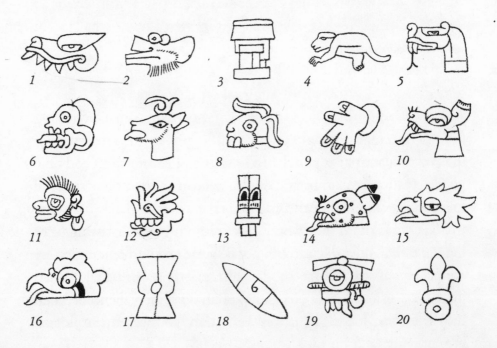

Priests kindle a flame at the New Fire Ceremony, which took place every fifty-two years, the sacred cycle of Aztec time.

day names. By combining each of the 13 numbers with each of the 20 day names the Aztecs could get 260 different combinations (13 × 20 = 260).

In addition to this calendar the Aztecs had an eighteen-month calendar that marked the solar year. In this solar calendar each month contained 20 days. As 20 × 18 = 360, the Aztecs added five "useless" or "unlucky" days to round out the solar year. Children born during the useless days were given Aztec names that meant "worthless," or "will never amount to anything."

The Aztec calendar round was made by imagining that the two calendars were intermeshed cogged wheels — one with 260 cogs and the other with 365 cogs. The sacred period of time, according to the Aztecs, was fifty-two years — the amount of revolutions it took for a particular cog in the 365-cog wheel to mesh a second time with a particular cog in the 260-cog wheel, and for the days once more to repeat themselves in their original order. Each fifty-two-year cycle closed with a New Fire Ceremony. On the last night of the cycle the Aztecs, fearing that the world would be devoured by monsters, put out all their fires, smashed their pottery, and cleaned their houses. Some of them gathered anxiously on the hillsides to watch the heavens with the priests. At a certain moment a tiny new

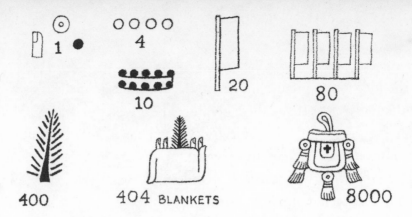

The Aztec numbering system. (From the Codex Mendoza.*)*

fire was kindled on the slashed chest of the victim to be sacrificed. From this flame, sacred-fire torches were lighted, and runners sped across the countryside carrying the precious fire to the people — a signal that life would go on for another fifty-two years.

Each of the eighteen months in the solar calendar was marked with special religious celebrations. The first month, Atlcoualco (atl-ko-*wahl*-ko), or "want of water," was celebrated with ceremonies, parades, and sacrifices. The celebration during the fourth month was in honor of the new corn. The eighth month brought the eight-day festival of eating ripened corn, and the sacrifice of a young girl who took the part of the corn goddess. Other months celebrated such things as the gift of rain, the war gods, the fall of the fruits, and the return of the gods to earth.

The Aztecs used a number system in estimating their calendars and in doing business. A dot or a finger meant one. Dots were used for numbers up to 20. The sign of a flag meant 20. A single feather stood for 400, and a bag with tassels for 8,000. The Aztecs, like the Maya, used a "base twenty," or vigesimal, number system, whereas we use the "base ten," or decimal, system.

In addition to picture numbers, the Aztecs used picture writing, or hieroglyphs, often called glyphs. The glyph for traveling was bare footprints; for war, a black sky and a closed eye; for victory, a burning temple pierced by a sword. Books, or codices, containing these colorful glyphs record wanderings, wars, kings, calendar counts, the sacred almanac, astronomy, astrology, and tribal events. Later, after the arrival of the Spaniards, the spoken literature of the Aztecs — their beautiful poetry-stories, hymns, prayers, and chants — was translated from the Nahuatl language and written for the first time. This spoken literature had been remembered and recited from generation to generation over countless years.

The paper used in Mixtec, Zapotec, and Aztec books came from the "paper tree," a wild fig tree. Sheets of the inner bark were stripped, soaked in water, and pounded with a stone. Later the paper was dried and coated with starch or other substances, to make it smooth and white. A long strip was then folded over and over like an accordion, and two thin boards, or perhaps animal skins, were fastened to the first and last pages. The paints used to illustrate the books were made from animal, vegetable, and mineral dyes.

The people of Mexico loved music and dancing. Although we do not know what their music sounded like, we do know that it was strongly rhythmic. Most of the musical instruments were rhythm instruments: drums of clay and wood with snakeskins or animal skins stretched over the top; notched bones, which were scraped with a stick to make a rasping noise; various kinds of rattles, whistles, and flutes. Both music and dancing were performed at religious ceremonies only.

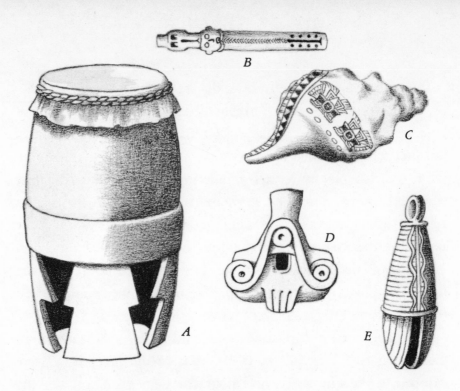

Aztec musical instruments. A. Huehuetl drum. B. Double flute (clay). C. Conch-shell horn. D. Whistle (clay). E. Copper bell.

Besides being skilled in literature, music, and dancing, the Aztecs were expert artists and craftsmen, although their work was not as fine as that of the Zapotecs, Mixtecs, Cholulans, and some other peoples of Central America. The *tolteca*, or artisans, sculptured in stone; carved figurines from stones such as rock crystal, turquoise, and jade; painted murals, or wall decorations; fashioned figures in clay; and later worked in gold and silver. The Aztecs considered jade the most precious of all stones.

Clay was also used for making fine pottery for religious uses, as well as for shaping everyday ware such as pots, bowls, cups, incense burners, dolls, and vases.

The finest pottery was made for the dead, for their use in the after-life. A. Polychrome (many-colored) bowl. B. Mortar. The inside bottom has a rough surface for grinding foods.

A

B

The people of Mexico at that time did not use a potter's wheel. Pottery was formed by working coils of clay with the hands, gradually building up the sides of the piece being made. By pasting on bits of clay or marking the piece with an obsidian knife, Mexican artists created many lovely decorations. In addition, fine pottery was painted in a variety of colors.

Almost no examples of Aztec architecture have been left for us to study, because the Spaniards destroyed Tenochtitlán. Much of what was once thought to be Aztec architecture is, in truth, the work of such fine builders as the Teotihuacans, the Zapotecs, and the Toltecs. Some temples now remaining in Mexico were built during the Aztec period, however, so that we have an idea of what the Aztec architecture was like.

TENOCHTITLAN

On November 12, 1519, four days after entering Tenochtitlán, Cortés and his captains were invited to climb the 114 steps to the top of the great temple that stood in the great square of Tlaltelolco. There Montezuma took Cortés by the hand, according to Díaz del Castillo, and "told him to look at his great city and all the other cities that were standing in the water, and the many other towns on the land round the lake. . . . So we stood looking about us, for that huge and cursed temple stood so high that from it one could see over everything very well, and we saw the three causeways which led into Mexico . . . and we saw the fresh water that comes from Chapultepec which supplies the city, and we saw the bridges on the three causeways . . . and we beheld on that great lake a great multitude of canoes, some coming with supplies of food and others returning loaded with cargoes of merchandise . . . and we saw that . . . it was impossible to pass from house to house, except by drawbridges which were made of wood or in canoes; and we saw in those cities Cues [temples] and oratories like towers and fortresses and all gleaming white, and it was a wonderful thing to behold. . . ."

Behind the Spaniards, on the pyramid's platform, stood the double shrine to the two great gods Huitzilopochtli and Tezcatlipoca, They were allowed to enter. Within the right-hand door stood the squat stone figure of Huitzilopochtli, covered with precious stones, gold, pearls, and seed pearls. About his waist was a belt of great snakes made of gold and precious stones and around his neck hung

54

Stone sacrificial knife with a mosaic handle representing an Eagle Knight.

a string of gold masks and silver hearts inlaid with turquoise. There were braziers and in them were burning incense and the hearts of three Indians who had recently been sacrificed. The walls and floors were black with the blood of many victims. According to Díaz del Castillo, the shrines smelled like slaughterhouses, and the battle-toughened Spaniards anxiously waited to leave.

On that day the Spaniards viewed the greatest city in the Americas, a city of from 300,000 to 500,000 people that covered approximately 2,500 acres. Below them in the great square was the marketplace, crowded with from 25,000 to 60,000 people. Díaz del Castillo wrote, "We were astounded at the number of people and the quantity of merchandise that it contained, and at the good order and control that was maintained, for we had never seen such a thing before."

The market in the great square at Tlaltelolco was larger than that in the main square at Tenochtitlán. Both were conducted in like manner, however. Each kind of goods was always located in the same place and in neat rows. Díaz del Castillo tells that gold, silver, precious stones, feathers, mantles, and embroidered goods were kept together. Next came the slaves who were for sale, some tied to poles, and some not. Then there were the traders in cloth and cotton. Cacao, or chocolate, was sold in another row. In other parts of the

This great plumed serpent's head was at the base of the ramp by the stairs leading up to the temple of Huitzilopochtli and Tlaloc — the most magnificent temple in Tenochtitlán. It was found during recent excavations on the edge of the great square in Mexico City.

market there were row after row of fruits, vegetables, meats, pottery, sweets made of honey paste, paper, colors for dyeing cloth and for writing, herbs, oil-bearing seeds, salt, the skins of pumas and jaguars and foxes, knives of obsidian and flint, lumber, firewood, copper axes, rare flowers. "But why do I waste so many words in recounting what they sell in that great market?" wrote Díaz del Castillo, "— for I shall never finish if I tell it all in detail."

According to Cortés, stalls in the marketplace sold "medicines ready to be taken, ointments and poultices. There are barbershops, where one can be washed and trimmed; there are houses where, upon payment, one may eat and drink."

Soldiers policed the marketplaces. When a dispute arose, the opponents were taken to a court at one end of the area. Here three

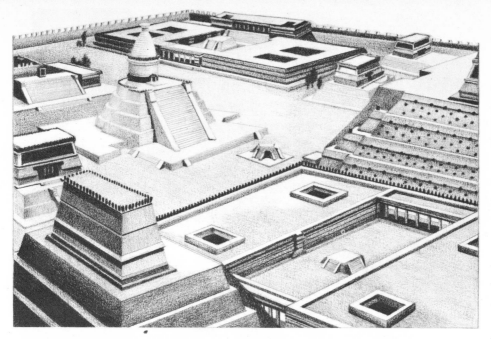

Tenochtitlán's religious center was enclosed by the "Wall of Serpents." The round temple was dedicated to Quetzalcóatl. Almost in the middle of the picture is a low platform which once supported a large stone. A prisoner was tied to the center of this stone and given wooden weapons with which to defend himself against six other warriors armed with real weapons. If he defeated them, an unlikely chance, he was freed and held in high esteem.

judges took turns in handing down on-the-spot verdicts. The punishment for stealing in the marketplace or for highway robbery was instant death by stoning. A common thief was put into slavery until he had worked off the amount stolen or had paid back double what he had taken. Aztec laws were harsh, and punishment swift.

The main temple court of Tenochtitlán lay within the "Wall of Serpents," so called because it was decorated on the outside by figures of serpents. The colossal twin pyramid-temple to Huitzilopochtli and Tlaloc dominated the square. Within the walls was the round temple to the great god Quetzalcóatl, God of Life and Learning, and of the Wind. Its door was carved and painted to resemble a serpent's mouth. Ball courts, raised altars, skull racks, and other temples filled this religious city. Beyond the "Wall of Serpents" was the beautiful palace of Montezuma. This huge building could be reached either on foot or by boat, for Tenochtitlán was truly another Venice — a city of canals, lagoons, and fingers of water spanned by bridges and causeways.

According to Díaz del Castillo, "The great Montezuma was about forty years old, of good height and well proportioned, slender and spare of flesh. . . . He did not wear his hair long, but so just to cover his ears. His scanty black beard was well-shaped and thin. His face was somewhat long, but cheerful, and he had good eyes and showed in his appearance and manner often tenderness and when necessary, gravity. He was very neat and clean and bathed once every day in the afternoon."

His palace, with its many halls and luxurious rooms, was filled with people even at dawn, for this was when the Aztec day began. Government officials, singers, dancers, clowns, dwarfs, a host of servants, even artists and craftsmen, all waited to be summoned — to consult with or to amuse their king.

Within the palace walls were treasure rooms, kitchens, storage rooms, hanging gardens, a zoo containing jaguars and pumas, an aviary filled with rare tropical birds, and lagoons edged with beautiful flower and herb gardens.

Other handsome palaces and public buildings stood beyond the walls of the religious center, facing on the great square. Like Montezuma's, their walls were painted and sculptured in a myriad of designs and colors. Beyond the marketplace and great square were local temples and the white, one-storied houses of lesser officials, merchants, craftsmen, and the common people. These houses faced canals and footpaths, which were built side by side. The houses were windowless, but at the back of each was a court filled with flowers and vegetables.

Three raised causeways led from Tenochtitlán to the mainland, and according to Cortés they were wide enough for eight horsemen to ride abreast. In addition, these roads served as dikes, and they were broken every so often and the openings were spanned by wooden bridges. These openings prevented the lake water from piling up behind the dikes when the waves were high.

The rhythm of life for the Aztecs of Tenochtitlán was as steady and sure as the beat of the great snakeskin drum atop the Temple of Huitzilopochtli, which sounded nine times a day. The people poled their dugouts along the canals or padded barefoot along the earth-packed streets to work, to the markets, the temples, the schools, and the great public religious ceremonies.

Today Tenochtitlán lies buried about 30 feet below Mexico City. The lake in which it once stood has dried up. The main square of the modern city lies almost exactly over Tenochtitlán's great square. The palace of the President of the Republic of Mexico is built above Montezuma's palace. Not far from the modern Cathedral, the remains of the base of the magnificent temple to Huitzilopochtli have been found. In 1519 this pyramid-temple did not resemble the first rude temple built by the Tenochcas when they founded their nation. Succeeding kings had built larger and more magnificent temples over the first one. The practical Aztecs, and other Mexican peoples, filled in and built over existing temples as a matter of course.

The Aztec Calendar Stone is thirteen feet in diameter. In the center is the sign representing the present era, "Four Motion." Day names, signs indicating precious things, the sun's rays, star symbols, and finally, two fire snakes symbolizing time appear in the other circles. This stone was found beneath the great square in Mexico City, and is now in the National Museum of Anthropology.

Gold ornament repre-senting the Aztec uni-verse. At the top the gods are playing ball. Below is a sun disk, a knife symbolizing the moon, and an earth mon-ster. At the bottom are four decorative pendants.

The earth beneath the modern square is filled with countless treasures that may never be recovered, due to the danger of weakening existing foundations by digging. Nonetheless, this area has produced priceless treasures, among them the famous Aztec Calendar Stone and the hideous statue of the mother goddess Coatlicue, "the Lady of the Serpent Skirts."

THE SPANISH CONQUISTADORES

Cortés and his tiny army had fought off thousands of Indians on their way from the Gulf Coast, over two hundred miles away. They had suffered from hunger, wounds, and exhaustion. With a force of four hundred Spaniards and about one thousand Indian allies, Cortés planned to conquer a nation that could easily put one hundred thousand warriors in the field.

Why did Montezuma allow the Spaniards to approach his capital without a battle? Why did he even welcome them?

There are many reasons. The most important one is that Montezuma believed Cortés to be the great god Quetzalcóatl, come to reclaim his people and lands. Quetzalcóatl was thought to have left his country many years before, on a raft of intertwined snakes. The date of his departure was *ce acatl*. He promised to return on another *ce acatl*. The year 1519, the year the Spaniards arrived, was a *ce acatl* year, according to the Aztec calendar. In addition, Quetzal-

Cortés' route from the Gulf of Mexico to Tenochtitlán.

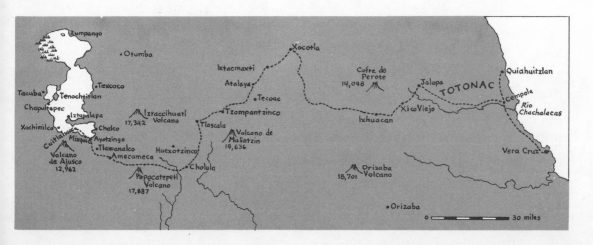

Quetzacóatl as the Wind God. He is shown wearing a mask shaped like a bird's beak.

cóatl was thought to be white and bearded. Cortés was also white and bearded.

Another reason Montezuma was unable to act against the invaders was that the Aztecs had never seen horses, cannons, muskets, crossbows, or the huge mastiff dogs who fought by the side of their Spanish masters. All these things were mysterious and frightening to the Indians.

Finally, the Aztecs were having trouble with several tribes near the Gulf Coast, for these tribes deeply resented paying tribute to Tenochtitlán. The rebels welcomed the Spaniards as liberators and became their allies.

Montezuma had tried bribing the Spaniards. In a vain attempt to keep Cortés from coming to Tenochtitlán, he had sent his ambassadors with rich gifts of gold, silver, jade, embroidered cloths, and a magnificent feather headdress. But the more the Spaniards saw of these riches, the more certain they were that Tenochtitlán must be theirs.

A certain Indian woman, Marina, played a large part in the downfall of the Aztecs. She had been given as a slave to Cortés and was devoted to him. Understanding both the Nahuatl and Mayan languages, she quickly picked up Spanish. For her master she worked cleverly on the superstitious nature of the Indians. There were as many intrigues as there were battles between the Spaniards and the various Indian tribes. In time, the Spanish were able to gain as allies the powerful Totonacs and Tlaxcalans.

Cortés and his small army entered Tenochtitlán on November 8, 1519. They were greeted cordially by Montezuma and his nobles and were conducted to the palace of Montezuma's deceased father, which faced the great square. For a week the Spaniards spent their time sightseeing in the splendid city, then Cortés took Montezuma prisoner. For many months the Spaniard ruled the Aztecs through their captive king. Then Cortés left Tenochtitlán for the Gulf Coast, to put down a rebellion led by one of his own countrymen.

In his absence his lieutenant, Alvarado, attacked a group of Aztecs who had gathered for a feast, and killed them all. The people of Tenochtitlán rose up against the Spaniards and drove them to seek refuge within the walls of their quarters. For some strange reason the Aztecs permitted Cortés and a new force to enter the

Cortés meets Montezuma and his nobles. The conquistador is probably speaking English to Marina who, in turn is translating into Nahuatl for Montezuma. (From the Codex Florentino.)

city to join the beleaguered troops. When Montezuma tried to quiet his people, they stoned him to death, according to most reports, though some reports claim he was murdered by the Spaniards. The siege of the palace lasted a week before the Spaniards attempted a break. But their early-dawn escape was seen by a woman drawing water from a canal. She raised the alarm and the battle was on. Because they were weighted down with the gold they had stolen, many of the Spaniards died while trying to swim the short distance to the mainland.

The Spanish loss would have been greater still, had not the Aztecs stopped to recover their riches from the bodies of the dead and dying Spaniards.

After resting his troops and rallying new ones, Cortés launched several campaigns around the countryside. Soon the Texcocans, lifelong allies of the Aztecs, swung over to the Spanish side. Their city gave the Spaniards a base on Lake Texcoco and a new chance to defeat the Aztecs. Cortés ordered brigantines to be built and armed with cannons. Once ready, these boats, which also carried musketeers and crossbowmen, quickly reduced the number of war canoes on the lake, and the Spaniards set about the task of invading the island city.

Now the Aztecs began to fight for their lives. Cortés soon realized that the only way to take Tenochtitlán was to destroy it gradually, filling in the canals with the rubble so that he might build the ground necessary for maneuvering his cavalry and artillery. Each day the Aztecs saw more of their beautiful city pulled down. Weakened by colds, by hunger, and by smallpox and measles — hitherto unknown diseases brought by the Spaniards — the Aztecs gradually lost their will to resist. Finally Cuauhtémoc (kwow-*tay*-mok), the new king, attempted to flee with his family in a canoe. They were picked up by one of Cortés' brigantines, and were taken to the Spanish leader. Cuauhtémoc was later imprisoned and finally was put to death.

The Aztecs could not cope with the European method of warfare: prolonged battles, siege, destruction, and killing. They were accustomed to short wars whose main purpose was to capture prisoners. The religion that had forged a mighty state contained the seeds of its destruction. Two worlds had clashed, neither understanding the other's warfare, worship, or way of life. The Aztec nation fell after seventy-five days of fighting, on August 13, 1521.

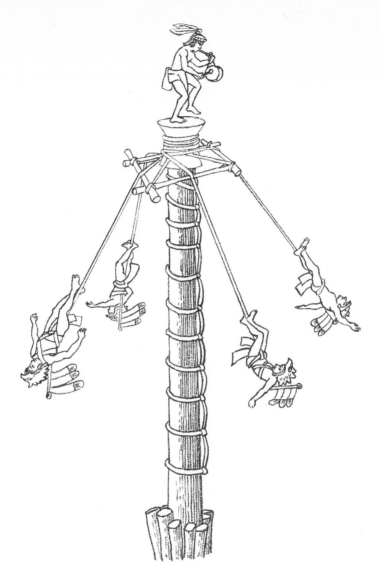

One Aztec ceremony still being performed today in Mexico took place at the Volador, or "Flying Place." Four men dressed as gods in bird forms and tied by ropes to the pole flung themselves backward from the platform. The captain stood beating a small drum. The "birds" waved their arms like wings and soared thirteen times around the pole before reaching the ground. Thirteen turns x 4 flyers = 52, the sacred cycle of Aztec time.

INDEX